BLM

Idaho
National Landscape
Conservation System Strategy
2012-2015

© James Neeley

The Geography of Hope

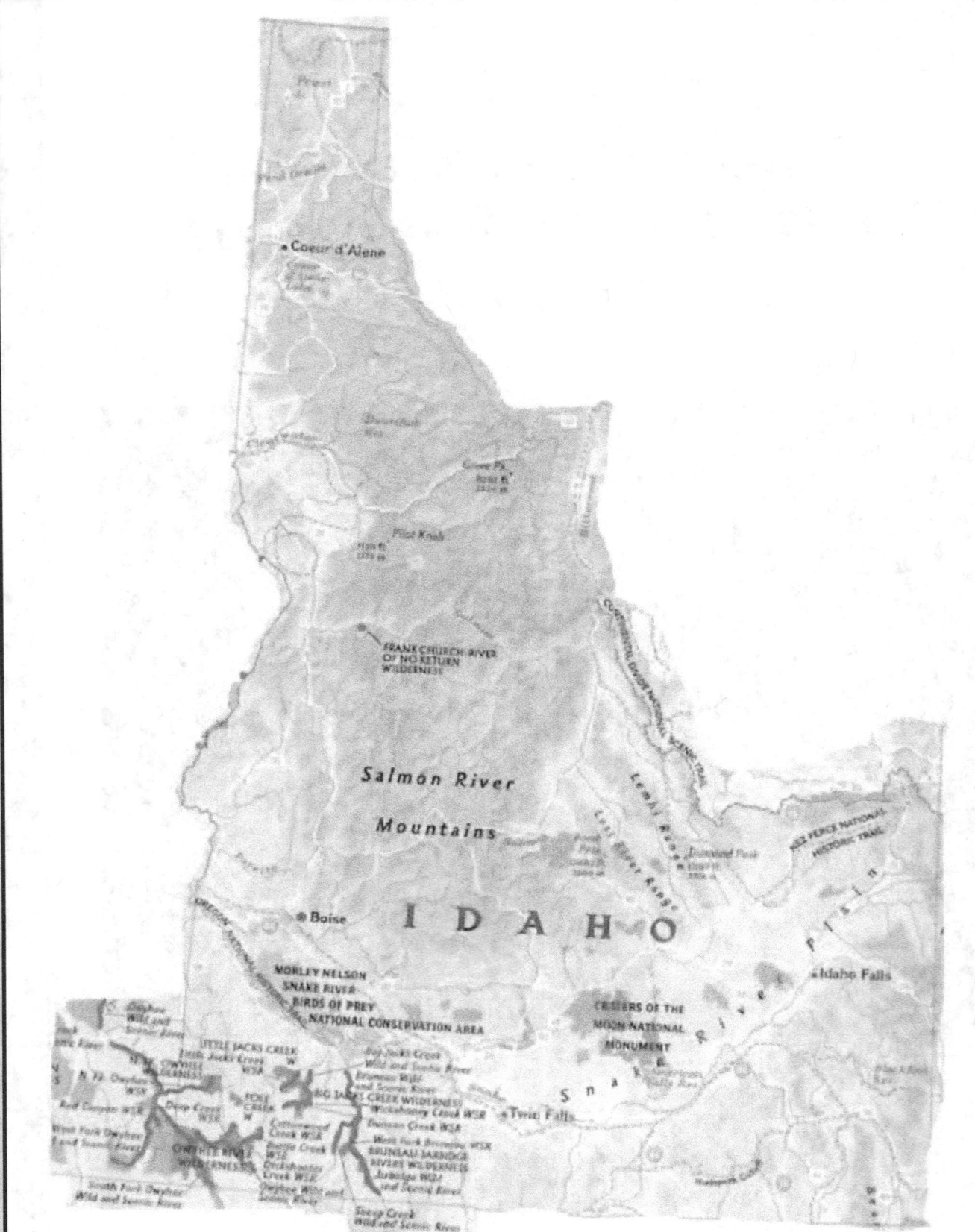

Idaho NLCS State Strategy

Congress has provided the Bureau of Land Management (BLM) the privilege of protecting many special places for a myriad of uses. Of these lands and waters, those of the National Landscape Conservation System (NLCS) have been set aside specifically for conservation, preservation, and restoration. Established in 2000, this System represents a new multiple use conservation paradigm for the 21st Century, one that emphasizes landscapes capable of sustaining ecosystems and recreation while balancing the Bureau's support for commodity users and consumers here and around the world. This System is managed in a way that enriches and responds to a contemporary American culture's evolving needs and has the unique capacity to adapt and remain contemporary.

Morley Nelson Snake River Birds of Prey National Conservation Area

The NLCS offers some of the most remarkable and expansive landscapes found on public lands in the American West. To be a component of the NLCS, a unit must have been designated for protective and conservation purposes by the Congress or President. The System focuses on the opportunities and management needs of these national treasures. The landscapes often preserve parts of our nation's diverse national heritage. Managing these areas is part of the BLM's multiple use mission to sustain the health of the public lands for present and future generations.

The Bureau of Land Management's NLCS Strategy supports: 1) conservation, protection and restoration; 2) communities and partnerships; 3) science; and 4) visitor services throughout the System. These four goals constitute the foundation for a new conservation vision for the twenty-first century based upon the BLM's unique multiple use mission.

The national NLCS program released the "National Landscape Conservation System 15-Year Strategy" in 2011. The strategy focused on four themes, each with multiple goals, objectives, and actions. One of the actions was for each state to develop their own NLCS strategy. This Idaho-specific strategy is consistent with the national strategy and focuses on the same four themes. Idaho's strategy is intended to provide direction for the NLCS program for the next three to five years.

Craters of the Moon National Monument and Preserve

This strategy applies to the following NLCS lands administered by the Bureau:

	Boise District	Twin Falls District	Idaho Falls District	Coeur d'Alene District
National Monuments & National Conservation Areas	Morley Nelson Snake River Birds of Prey National Conservation Area	Craters of the Moon National Monument and Reserve		
National Scenic and Historic Trails	Oregon National Historic Trail	Oregon National Historic Trail California National Historic Trail	Nez Perce National Historic Trail Lewis and Clark National Historic Trail Continental Divide National Scenic Trail Oregon National Historic Trail California National	Nez Perce (Nee-Me-Poo) National Historic Trail
Wilderness Areas	Pole Creek N. Fork Owyhee Owyhee River Big Jacks Creek Little Jacks Creek Bruneau-Jarbidge Rivers	Bruneau-Jarbidge Rivers		
Wilderness Study Areas	Two WSAs	Eighteen WSAs	Twenty-one WSAs	Four WSAs
Wild and Scenic Rivers	Sixteen Wild and Scenic Rivers (325 miles)			

Theme 1 *Ensuring the Conservation, Protection, and Restoration of NLCS Values*

The NLCS lands are designated by Congress or the President to conserve, protect, and restore their unique values for the benefit of current and future generations. As such, there is an overarching and explicit commitment to conservation and resource protection as the primary objective within these areas. In this theme, we focus on ensuring that BLM management of NLCS lands is guided by the purposes for which the lands were designated and on using science to further conservation, protection, and restoration of these landscapes, while providing opportunities for compatible public use and enjoyment.

Oregon National Historic Trail wagon replica

Goal 1 Ensuring the Conservation, Protection, and Restoration of NLCS Values.

1. Primacy of conservation within the NLCS, how science serves to further conservation, and to provide for compatible use that protects NLCS resources and values.

Goal 1A Clearly communicate that the conservation, protection, and restoration of NLCS values is the highest priority in NLCS planning and management, consistent with the designating legislation or presidential proclamation.

Overall Actions

1. Idaho will use guidance provided in Manual 6100 to ensure that designating legislation and proclamation are the highest priority in managing NLCS units.

2. Ensure Idaho land-use plans and environmental review documents address NLCS values.

3. Ensure land use plan amendments and implementation/activity level plans are consistent with the designating legislation or proclamation.

4. Promote use of challenge cost share.

5. Identify National Scenic & Historic Trail corridors consistent with manual guidance.

6. Establish land acquisition and transfer priorities to acquire lands from willing sellers through land exchange, purchase, donation, and similar methods (outside legislated land exchanges).

7. Coordinate and prioritize NLCS budget proposals that fulfill strategy priorities.

State Level Actions

1. Develop measures and conduct periodic management reviews to assess management effectiveness of National Monuments (NMs) and National Conservation Areas (NCAs). Apply results of the reviews to adaptively improve management and share best practices.

South Fork Owyhee Wild & Scenic River

2. State Office will conduct management reviews of the NCA/NM (a minimum of every five years). The results of these reviews will be used to improve existing management.

3. State Office program leads should ensure coordinated budget planning to support NLCS priorities.

Unit Level Actions

1. Develop a stand-alone land-use plan for NMs and NCAs that conforms with the primacy of the designating legislation or proclamation for all parts of the NLCS in planning and management.

2. Idaho has completed stand-alone Resource Management Plans for Craters of the Moon National Monument and Birds of Prey NCAs. As needed, these land use plans will be either revised or amended to address specific issues.

3. In coordination with other BLM programs, establish conservation priorities for each NLCS unit based on the mandates of the designating legislation or proclamation and coordinate funding to maximize conservation benefits.

4. Ensure NCA and NM management plans explicitly define legislation or proclamation objects and values, and those plans contain desired future conditions and management actions that contribute to the protection or enhancement of those objectives and values.

5. Ensure that each new management plan completes an implementation strategy and updates that strategy every five years.

6. Ensure that visual resource management classes are consistent with the values of the legislation or proclamation.

Goal 1B&C **Expand a science based foundation for decision making through assessment, inventory, and monitoring.**

Overall Actions

1. Wherever possible, work with partners and volunteers to conduct assessment, inventory, and monitoring of NLCS areas. Ensure that assessment, inventory, and monitoring data are readily available to BLM management and staff, scientists, and the general public.

    a. State Office and Field Offices identify partners/volunteers and identify/develop monitoring protocols specific for each type of NLCS unit.

    b. Enhance the role of science partnerships in resource management and the engagement of the public to assist with scientific work (citizen science).

State Level Actions

1. Cadastral survey will provide support for identifying boundaries of NLCS units.

2. Continue to provide geospatial data on Inside Idaho website.

3. Implement the NLCS Science Research Program, addressing BLM data gaps to facilitate management decisions.

4. Communicate internally and externally and integrate the results of scientific research and studies on NLCS lands.

5. Work with BLM's Riparian Service Team, National Operating Center (NOC), the BLM Science Advisor, and others for timely research/studies within the NLCS.

6. Share resulting findings and best management practices throughout the BLM and with interested publics/organizations.

7. Provide consistent definitions of science-related terminology and concepts to facilitate technical transfer and understanding.

8. Develop a filing system for Wilderness Study Area (WSA) inventory monitoring reports.

Big Jacks Creek Wilderness

Unit Level Actions

1. In collaboration with federal, tribal, and state agencies and other BLM programs, develop or compile, and maintain baseline inventory and geo-referenced data of NLCS values.

   a. Compile and maintain digital baseline inventory database of objects, values, conditions, and trends that is readily available to staff and managers.

   b. Develop an annotated bibliography of scientific studies that have been completed for the different units.

   c. Develop an inventory and monitoring plan as part of the science strategy.

2. Conduct boundary assessments and compile geospatial data of NLCS area boundaries. Post boundary signs in high priority areas to inform the public and deter incompatible uses within NLCS lands.

b. Incorporate boundary assessments in monitoring strategies.

c. Idaho BLM will post signs at key access points for the different NLCS units.

3. Establish consistent protocols for monitoring NLCS values to better and more quickly inform management decisions and to assess operational effectiveness and performance.

a. Develop integrated monitoring strategies by unit (NCA/NM) or unit type (Wild & Scenic Rivers, National Scenic and Historic Trails).

b. Use the "Keeping It Wild" wilderness character monitoring reports to inform management decisions on impacts to wilderness character.

c. All designated wilderness areas will complete baseline wilderness character inventories according to established schedules, with all units completed in 2014.

d. All designated wilderness areas will conduct annual and five-year monitoring updates in accordance with BLM's Wilderness Character Monitoring Protocol.

e. WSA inventory reports will be utilized in project analyses, and annual monitoring will be conducted in accordance with BLM's WSA monitoring standards to ensure that actions do not "impair the suitability of such areas for preservation as wilderness."

Petroglyphs in the Wilderness

f. All NMs and NCAs will maintain an inventory of NLCS objects and values identified in their enabling legislation or proclamations, and from post-designation inventories and subsequent monitoring. Such values will receive priority for conservation, protection, and restoration in land use plans and subsequent implementation-level plans and projects.

g. WSRs will be monitored to ensure, protection, and enhancement of Outstandingly Remarkable Values identified for each designated river corridor.

h. National Scenic and Historic Trails (NSHTs) and study trails will be monitored to document the values and objects of each trail. This information will be included in corridor identification and management planning to ensure that future actions do not substantially interfere with such values and objects.

4. Develop and implement science strategies for NLCS areas (with emphasis on NMs, NCAs, and areas of special scientific importance) to identify research needs and incorporate physical, biological, and social science into management, decision-making, and outreach.

   a. Develop Idaho-specific science goals by area/administrative unit.

   b. Continue to develop science research proposals and apply for research grants.

5. Promote the NLCS to universities and research institutions as a major research resource consistent with the protection of NLCS values. Emphasize projects that meet identified NLCS research needs.

   a. Promote science workshops within NLCS units.

   b. Effectively utilize existing state and national networks to support research and share scientific information.

   c. Develop relationships with Idaho and other universities to encourage research within NLCS units.

6. To the extent consistent with NLCS unit's conservation and protection goals, all units will support scientific research aimed at improving management of the unit and offering important findings relevant to public land management beyond the borders of the units themselves.

   a. Scientific research reports will be highlighted and made available on the BLM website.

Goal 1D   Use the NLCS as an outdoor laboratory and demonstration center for new and innovative management and business processes.

State Level Actions

1. Promote opportunities to share practices (for example, online forums, publications, training, workshops, conferences) for application to NLCS and other BLM lands.

   a. Encourage increased use of NLCS units for scientific research and require a formal report following completion of scientific research.

   b. Use BLM's Daily to promote and highlight successful projects.

   c. Use social media outlets (Facebook, Twitter, YouTube, etc.) to highlight projects to the public.

Goal 1E   **Authorize only those discretionary uses that are compatible with the NLCS unit's legislation or proclamation.**

State Level Actions

1. Develop protocol for assessing compatibility of future proposed uses.

Unit Level Actions

1. Identify existing and potential uses that are compatible with the designating legislation or presidential proclamation.

   a. Identify incompatible uses during development of the Resource Management Plan (RMP) and other unit management plans.

   b. Utilize compatibility protocol when considering future project proposals.

2. Work with the holders of valid existing rights to limit negative impacts to NLCS values.

3. Use the best available science to conduct capacity studies, establish specific, measurable, attainable, relevant, and time-specific (SMART) objectives (or similar), and develop monitoring plans for compatible uses to ensure the NLCS values are protected, consistent with the designating legislation or presidential proclamation. Use the monitoring results to make decisions and adaptively manage the compatible uses so they are not in conflict with NLCS values.

4. Where NLCS units have a high conservation value in a broader context for a species population or ecosystem health, utilize NLCS units for mitigation for projects occurring outside the units, so that conservation efforts outside NLCS units can build upon efforts within the units in order to protect the entire species population or ecosystem.

Dedication Point overlook Birds of Prey NCA

   a. State Office develop/provide guidance on applicability of mitigation for projects inside and outside of NLCS units.

5. Collaborate with partners and stakeholders to complete and implement travel management plans for each NM and NCA within five years of completion of the land use plan. Provide for public access and opportunities (e.g., trails), including the needs of persons with disabilities while protecting resources.

   a. Utilize partnerships to leverage funding and support for the development and implementation of travel management plans.

   b. Apply for discretionary transportation funding to support travel management planning efforts.

   c. Maximize the use of grant opportunities to implement travel management plans.

Goal 1F   **Manage facilities in a manner that promotes, conserves, protects, and restores NLCS values.**

State Level Actions

1. State Office will use BLM's Guidelines for a Quality Built Environment to direct design and construction of facilities.

Unit Level Actions

1. Consider development of visitor or information centers within local communities to foster stewardship, contribute to the local economy, provide for public safety and enjoyment, and minimize development within NLCS areas.

2. NCA staff will work with the State, City of Kuna, World Center Birds of Prey, Celebration Park, and other partners to support existing infrastructure that provide NCA information to the public.

    a. Expand use of social media and websites to disseminate information.

    b. Craters NM staff will continue to support the Craters National Park Service visitor center.

    c. Craters NM will work with the City of Carey to provide public information.

    d. Work with chambers of commerce, state and federal agencies to provide information on individual NLCS units.

3. The BLM will only develop facilities, including roads, on NLCS lands where they are required for public health and safety, are necessary for the exercise of valid existing rights, minimize impacts to fragile resources, or further the purposes for which an area was designated.

    a. Development of facilities will be addressed in RMPs or NLCS plans during planning process.

    b. New roads or trails would be addressed in a comprehensive travel management plan for the NCA or NM or in the Owyhee Wilderness Management Plan.

4. Remove abandoned, dilapidated, or unneeded federal facilities and structures that do not possess cultural or historic significance and restore the areas those facilities occupied.

   a. Abandoned or unneeded facilities will be identified and their removal addressed in land use plans and appropriate RMPs.

   b. Within the NCA and NM these facilities will be addressed on a case by case basis.

Theme 2 *Collaboratively Managing the NLCS as Part of the Larger Landscape*

Recognizing that the NLCS represents a small portion of the land managed by the BLM and other federal, state, tribal, and local government entities. These special conservation areas must be managed within the context of the larger landscape. By establishing connections across boundaries with other jurisdictions, management of NLCS areas will complement conservation areas within the respective jurisdictions of the National Park

Bruneau River Phlox Bruneau WSR

Service, the Fish and Wildlife Service Refuge System, the U.S. Forest Service, state, tribal and local governments, and private conservation lands.

Collaborative management is critical component of managing at a landscape level. A collaborative landscape approach to NLCS management expands the support for BLM and increases the opportunities to promote healthy landscapes and appropriate land uses and to contribute to the local economy and social fabric of the community.

Goal 2A   Emphasize an ecosystem-based approach to manage the NLCS in the context of the surrounding landscape.

Overall Actions

1. Idaho BLM will work with other land management agencies and tribes to identify and participate in the opportunities to increase habitat connectivity to provide for sustainable populations of native species, especially where these species are either threatened and endangered species or are candidate species for listing.

State Level Actions

2. Idaho BLM's Rapid Eco-regional Assessments (REAs) and Regional Sage Grouse Environmental Impact Statement (EIS) will identify areas where NLCS units (Craters of Moon NM, Birds of Prey NCA, designated wilderness areas, etc.) are important for resource protection and conservation within a broader landscape context, such as providing for protection of sage grouse habitat, large-scale wildlife corridors, and water-dependent resources.

Unit level actions

3. Field Offices will work with tribes to manage and preserve cultural resources within the context of the cultural landscape and adjoining lands to provide the greatest conservation benefit.

Goal 2B   Adopt a cross-jurisdictional, community-based approach to landscape-level conservation planning and management.

State Level Actions

1. Field Offices will coordinate across all BLM programs to more efficiently achieve common program goals based on a common understanding of the designating legislation or presidential proclamation for a particular NLCS area.

    a. NLCS staff will work to internally highlight and expand the understanding of the primary values of the NLCS units they manage.

    b. Encourage staff to provide NLCS presentations at all employee meetings to enhance awareness of the goals and mission of the NLCS.

2. BLM will work to engage partners, stakeholders, and the public early in the planning process.

   a. Environmental assessments and land use plan revisions will be highlighted on Field Office websites and on social media sites.

   b. NLCS managers will personally contact organizations or individuals to encourage their participation in planning endeavors.

3. To the extent feasible, BLM will use existing collaborative forums to engage tribal, local, state, and other federal government agencies and members of the public in NLCS planning and management.

   a. Field Offices will coordinate with their local Resource Advisory Councils (RACs) on proposals for significant projects within NLCS units.

   b. Field Offices will consult with tribes to engage them in planning and management of NLCS units.

4. Idaho BLM will continue to use "Inside Idaho" (the state clearinghouse for geographic data) to provide geospatial data to the public and other entities.

Lower Salmon Suitable River near Snow Hole WSA

5. Work with tribes, partners and communities to understand the effects of NLCS management and planning on adjacent lands, including social, economic, and ecological impacts. Participate in local planning and watershed analyses efforts to identify the effects of adjacent land management on NLCS areas.

Goal 2C **Work with Congress, tribes, other federal and state agencies, and national and local communities to identify and protect lands that are critical to the long-term ecological sustainability of the landscape.**

Overall actions

1. Utilize existing large-scale assessments and maps, such as BLM's REAs, Sage-Grouse preliminary priority habitat, identified big horn sheep populations, and other wildlife corridor mapping efforts, wilderness inventories, and other federal and state agency analyses to inform collaborative planning and land acquisition efforts.

2. BLM can serve as an information resource for grassroots efforts interested in exploring possible designations through legislation pertaining to the NLCS and will encourage proposal supporters to include and work with diverse interest groups.

Continental Divide National Scenic Trail and Lemhi Pass

State Level Actions

1. BLM will use the REAs to develop a map identifying key habitat linkages between NLCS units in order to manage NLCS units within the larger-scale ecosystem and meet broad-scale conservation goals.

2. Idaho BLM will give higher priority to Land and Water Conservation Fund proposals that enhance ecological connectivity and that protect nationally significant landscapes with outstanding cultural, ecological, or scientific values.

3. Idaho will continue to work on the Owyhee land exchange with the State of Idaho for the purpose of enhancing the six wilderness areas in southwestern Idaho.

Unit Level Actions

Units will work with tribes to identify areas of mutual concern that are critical to long term ecological sustainability of the landscape.

Goal 2D   Adopt a community-based approach to recreation and visitor services delivery, consistent with the conservation purpose of the NLCS and the socio-economic goals of the local community.

Overall

1. BLM will utilize the annual visitor satisfaction survey which provides the BLM with both data for reporting results using national performance measures required under the Government Performance and Results Act (GPRA) of 1993 and information regarding visitors' satisfaction with value for fees paid. This survey also provides BLM site managers vital information relative to visitors' level of contentment with facilities, interpretation/education programs and materials, road/trail maintenance, staff service, and general recreation management.

State Level Actions

1. BLM Idaho will continue to actively participate in the Idaho Recreation and Tourism Initiative (IRTI). The IRTI is a coalition of state and federal agencies and others dedicated to providing Idaho citizens and visitors with expanded recreation opportunities. The primary objective is to improve public information and services associated with recreation and tourism opportunities in Idaho through partnerships and cooperation.

Gem State Grotto volunteers at Craters of the Moon NM

Unit Level Actions

1. Field Offices will support interagency visitor centers in gateway communities in conjunction with local entities (i.e., chambers of commerce) which provide "one-stop shopping" for visitors.

2. In addition to the current law enforcement agreements, Idaho BLM will seek to expand the use of law enforcement agreements where appropriate.

Theme 3   *Raising Awareness of the Value and Benefits of the BLM's NLCS*

This theme seeks to cultivate a sense of shared stewardship for the BLM-managed public lands and advance the relevance of conservation lands to communities of place and interest. The goals represent a multi-pronged approach to connect diverse groups of people, interests, and government organizations by building strong partnerships, attracting volunteers, engaging youth, and telling our story through education, interpretation, and outreach.

Goal 3A   **Launch a long-term public awareness initiative about the BLM's NLCS, including national and local outreach, communications, and media plans.**

Overall

1. Continue to support events that emphasize collaborative outreach and public awareness, such as National Public Lands Day and National Trails Day.

State Level Actions

Cave Draw, Bruneau-Jarbidge Rivers Wilderness

1. Inventory brochures, publications, and other outreach tools to determine what is currently available to the public about the NLCS. Identify and develop other needed outreach tools including but not limited to site-specific brochures, maps, websites, social media, and podcasts. Emphasize connections among local NLCS areas to the overall NLCS and the BLM system of public lands.

2. Use partners, social media, and websites to market NLCS units

3. Increase the use of the Internet and other available technologies to highlight recreation opportunities, offer reservations, and provide permits to recreation users.

Goal 3B   **Advance and strengthen partnerships to facilitate shared stewardship and to advance the relevance of the NLCS to communities of interest and place.**

State Level Actions

1. Develop and/or expand strategic partnerships, friends groups, and cooperating associations for the Morley Nelson Snake River Birds of Prey NCA and the Craters of the Moon NM and Preserve.

2. Identify learning opportunities such as Take It Outside activities, outfitter partnership trips on the Lower Salmon and the Cooper's Ferry interpretation effort on NLCS lands to enhance the awareness and understanding of NLCS lands in Idaho.

3. Work with Idaho Department of Tourism to promote NLCS units on their social media sites.

4. Work with Mountain Home Air Force Base, Idaho National Guard, and state and local organizations like Wykin Warriors, which serves veterans and military families to engage and involve them in activities on Idaho NLCS lands.

BLM mascot Seymour Antelope raises public awareness of the importance of connecting children with nature

5. Encourage employee development through participation in workshops and conferences that promote and foster partnerships.

Goal 3C   **Expand use of volunteers within the NLCS**

State Level Actions

1. Emphasize use of volunteers in Annual Work Plans.

2. Use Volunteer.gov and visitidaho.org "voluntourism" websites to recruit volunteers. Promote volunteer opportunities on Facebook and Twitter.

3. Provide volunteer training for employees.

Unit Level Action

1. Continue to work and expand partnerships with other agencies to leverage scarce resources available for volunteer programs.

2. Use youth corps and community service organizations for volunteer work, including Boy Scouts and school groups.

3. Provide BLM volunteer training in Idaho to maintain a knowledgeable cadre of volunteer coordinators. Recruit Master Naturalists to work on BLM projects.

4. Provide opportunities for the public to volunteer on NLCS lands. This could include trail projects in the wilderness areas, camp host positions, river clean-ups, restoration of closed roads, damaged areas, or building fences.

5. Work with local outdoor retailers like REI and Cabela's and others to support volunteer projects

Blue Heron

6. Continue to host NPLD events throughout the state. Encourage each NPLD project leader to provide a short primer to the participants on NLCS and how it fits within the BLM.

7. Work with non-profit organizations like American Hiking Society's Volunteer Vacation and Sierra Club's service project.

8. Work with "natural" partners like World Center for Birds of Prey to expand joint opportunities of mutual benefit.

Goal 3D   **Engage the public in stewardship of the NLCS through education and interpretation**

State Level Actions

1. Partner with statewide environmental and heritage education providers (Project Learning Tree, Project WILD, Project WET, Project Archaeology, etc.) to gain quality educational materials for use when featuring NLCS lands.

2. Partner with other agencies, educational institutions, or non-profits to produce tools such as podcasts and video clips to enhance distance learning opportunities.

3. Working with the BLM Idaho State Office environmental education staff, have Morley Nelson Snake River Birds of Prey NCA and the Craters of the

BLM employees visiting Big Jacks Creek Wilderness

Moon NM and Preserve develop education and interpretive plans.

4. Provide interpretive and educational tools, materials, and opportunities about the NLCS to commercial users and local landowners who in turn can help educate their employees and the public. Foster programs like "Partners Afloat" that educate outfitters and guides on the Lower Salmon River.

5. Increase public education and outreach to create awareness about our nation's cultural heritage and tribal interests and improve public understanding of the need to preserve cultural resources.

6. Continue support for existing programs such as *Tread Lightly!* and *Leave No Trace* to foster outdoor ethics and stewardship. Reinforce this stewardship message in publications and maps and with volunteer project participants.

7. Provide materials, photos, and movies for State Office Communications to keep the social media sites up to date and relevant to NLCS sites.

8. Produce materials for Junior Explorer program and use the program to highlight NLCS units.

Goal 3E **Recruit and retain well-trained youth from diverse backgrounds for entry-level careers, and engage youth in recreation, education, and stewardship on conservation lands.**

Unit Level Actions

1. Identify science and resource priorities that youth can address through long- or short-term assignments.

2. Increase participation in mentorship or other programs to provide information to youth on the NLCS and career pathways for BLM and land management conservation.

3. Partner with K-12, college, and graduate schools to assist with monitoring NLCS units, and design and deliver environmental education and interpretation programs.

4. Pursue and invite academic internships (those required for graduation in a specific program at high schools, colleges, universities, and law schools) to assist with NLCS planning and management at various levels.

Theme 4 *Building upon BLM Idaho's Commitment to Conservation*

This Theme outlines goals and actions to improve internal communication and facilitate intra-state coordination in a way that aligns and fully integrates the NLCS Program within BLM Idaho.

Goal 4A **Improve internal communication and understanding of the NLCS and its potential to enhance Idaho BLM as a whole.**

State Level Actions

1. Annually update and implement the Idaho NLCS Communication Plan.

2. Incorporate NLCS as a resource program in Land Use Planning efforts. Develop and provide a NLCS-Idaho presentation at staff meetings in each District.

3. Highlight Idaho NLCS projects on the BLM Daily, Idaho BLM in Action newsletter, and on social media.

4. Include NLCS information in new employee orientations.

5. Develop a job shadowing or short-term detail program that would encourage employee interaction with other NLCS staff.

6. Encourage Field Office managers to take staff (especially non-resource staff) out to NLCS units.

Goal 4B **Cultivate shared responsibility for the NLCS conservation mandate as an integral part of BLM Idaho's multiple-use, sustained-yield mission.**

State Level Actions

1. Ensure Idaho policy is consistent with national manual direction and policy across resource programs.

2. Continue to showcase with BLM staff the NLCS mission and its role in the larger BLM multiple use mission.

3. Leadership provides direction for interdisciplinary teams to understand and integrate NLCS guidance during planning and project analysis.

4. Encourage networking through NLCS workshops and webinars which focus on interdisciplinary projects and goals.

Goal 4C   Clearly define and justify staffing needs, and administratively organize the NLCS areas to operate as a cross-cutting program within Idaho BLM.

State Level Actions

1. Assess NLCS workloads and program direction in maintaining adequate staffing. Utilize staff expertise across the state in accomplishing NLCS unit priority workloads as funding allows.

2. Use implementation plans to identify NLCS staffing requirements.

3. Use targets and accomplishments and associated funding to justify staffing.

Goal 4D   Ensure the NLCS budget is coordinated with other resource programs. Set clear expectations and procedures for interdisciplinary budget development, priority setting, and reporting of accomplishments.

State Level Actions

1. Develop and maintain up-to-date implementation strategies for each NLCS unit or group of units based upon the approved Resource Management Plan. The implementation strategy will serve as the basis for interdisciplinary budget and workload development.

2. Communicate priority NLCS directives through the Planning Target Allocation (PTA) and Annual Work Plan (AWP).

3. Encourage the use of collaborative cost-share projects such as cooperative conservation initiatives, and other federal and non-federal programs to achieve management objectives for NLCS lands.

4. Provide grant writing training to Field Offices in conjunction with their partner organizations to leverage available funding opportunities and increase grant applications.

Morley Neslon Snake River Birds of Prey National Conservation Area

Bureau of Land Management

Idaho State Office

1387 S. Vinnell Way

Boise, Idaho 83709

208-373-4000